Thoughts Unspoken

Bhuvi Tibrewalla

To the ones with the thoughts in their heads

the dreams... and the nightmares

THOUGHTS UNSPOKEN

I am out with the lanterns,

Looking for myself.

~ Emily Dickinson

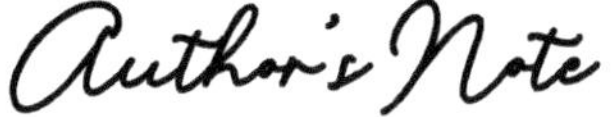

Author's Note

Poetries have always been my way of making sense of the world. Writing, for me, is a way of holding on to moments and this book is a piece of my heart, a collection of thoughts, stories, and wild hopes. I wrote it with the belief that words are bridges that bring us closer, helping us feel a little less lost, a little less alone. For me, finding my voice meant picking up a pen and letting it roar—or whisper, depending on the day. Whether it's scribbling down random thoughts in the middle of the night on a tissue paper or turning raw emotions into structured verse, writing is my playground.

These poems are where I unmask myself, peeling the layers to reveal the thoughts, fears, dreams, insecurities and vulnerabilities that don't always come out in daily life. Through these words, I explore the things I don't always say out loud—the questions, the inner battles, the wonder - The Thoughts Unspoken. So while I'm still that talkative, chirpy soul you see, my poetry is where I let my quieter self-speak. It's my way of balancing the two sides of me, where every poem tells a part of the story that goes unseen.

Welcome to my safe haven!

Here, the words meet feelings and silence speaks, it's a journey of love, loss and everything in between.

Playlist

"Mera safar" - Iqlipse Nova

"Hold on" – Chord Overstreet

"Ain't your mama"- Jennifer Lop

"We don't talk anymore"- Charlie Puth

"There's nothing holding me back" – Shawn Mendes

"Veere" – Vishal Mishra

"Pretty girl" – Maggie Lindemann

"Pick up the phone"- Henry Moodie

"Count on me" - Bruno Mars

"Aisa kyu maa" – Sunidhi Chauhan

"Unwritten" – Natasha Bedingfield

"I like me better" – Lauv

"Like my father" – Jax

"Kho gaye"- Jasleen Royal & Prateek Kuhad

THOUGHTS UNSPOKEN

Table of content

DISCOVERING HORIZONS

"You cannot swim for new horizons until you have courage to lose sight of the shore"

~ William Faulkner

Infinite Mirror of Belief

A barren canvas, a desolate stage,
each viewing it with varying perceptions,
embracing this subjective grace,
In truth and belief, they find their place.

Perception, a distorted kaleidoscope,
lens aligned properly,
through which we glimpse reality,
Pulling our minds due to gravity.

Through the Bible, Geeta, Quran, and many
more,
our beliefs and opinions are sown,
the threads of perception constrict our souls,
Forging the body, threads control.

Reality, a dissonant melody,
sunken into our souls,
A cacophony of thoughts, discordant and dwell,
Peers to truth, their stories swell.

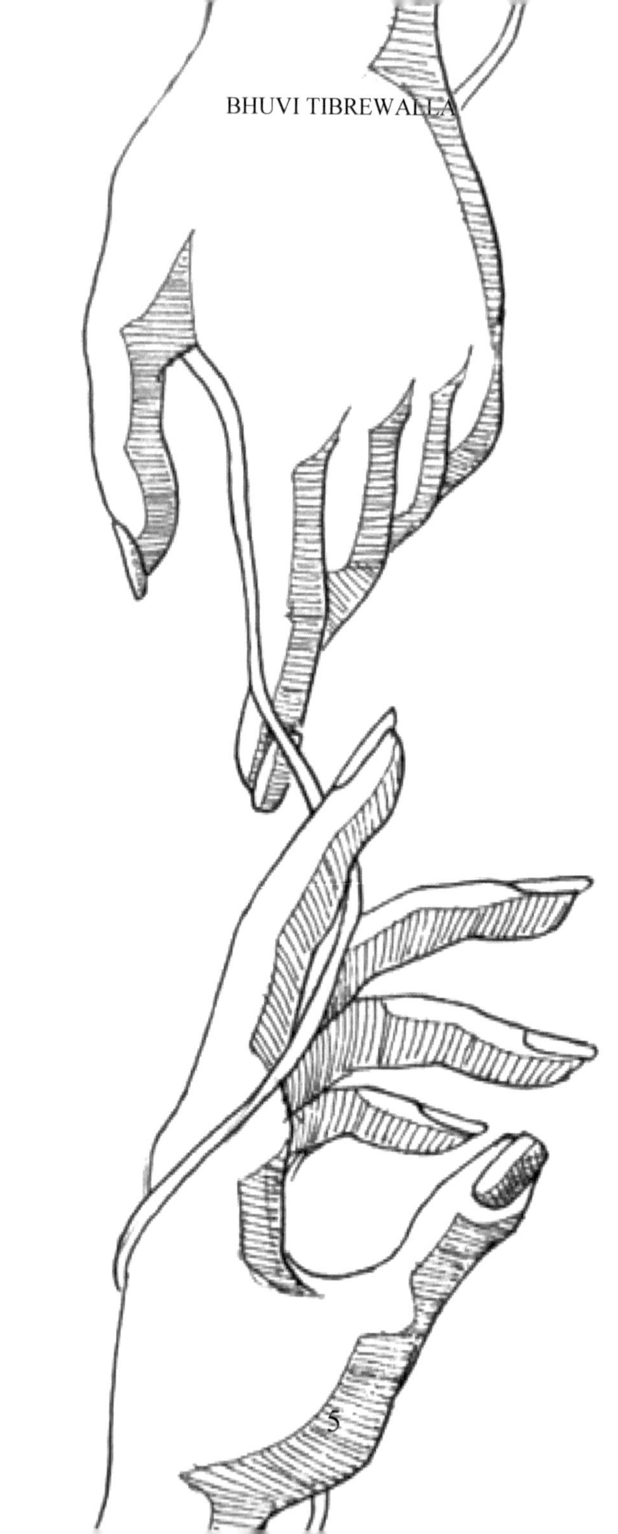
BHUVI TIBREWALLA

The Celestial Night

Last to last *night, a celestial sight,*

The moon and the star embraced the night,

The moon, radiant and glowing,

The star, quietly distanced, dreaming.

Last night I revisited the scene,

The star had taken its flight, serenely,

The moon stood there still,

looking at his beloved move away in frill,

The sky was adorned with twinkling vows,

as the promises they made echoed,

All just faded away,

like the depth of the night in a sway.

Today the star beams with cosmic might,

While the moon veiled itself from sight,

Bright stars persisted in cosmic might,

but the moon, once bright, lost its light.

On my terrace, today I stood,

Gazing up where the starlight stood,

The star shone all alone,

But the moon wasn't there anymore.

The World I Live In

This is the world I reside in,

A place where Cinderella may spurn the prince's side,

Where snow White can't toil with the dwarfs if she chooses to,

Where every girl is expected to have a happy ending like Belle and Ariel do,

She is forbidden to embrace Moana or Mirabel's guide of life.

A place where Barbie can't love Susie but has to love Ken,

Mulan constrained by her identity, can't pursue her desires,

Where a book is always judged by its cover,

And judgment matters more than reality,

A place where the inner self is neglected, like treasure cast aside.

In this sphere, I am ashamed to be in,

Where change remains elusive,

A world that will tell us to fly,

But then cut our wings and trap us inside.

It's full of superstitions, beliefs, and societies,

It will tell you to listen to others and drown the call to decide,

It will tell you to have a heart but yet be trapped in it,

It will tell you to sleep but not to dream.

It's a world where people will continue to be stuck in the constant,

A world reluctant to evolve,

This is the world I inhabit,

This is the world I am ashamed to reside in.

She

She is a piece of shattered glass,

For her being the reflection of gracefulness.

She is both the thunder and the calming rain.

She can be both peace and war.

For she they work,

For she they fear,

For she is her own kind,

She is perfect,

Yet so imperfect,

Like the curves of the body,

The scars on her skin,

The thoughts in her mind,

And the lines of her poetry.

For she is truthful beauty,

With divine elegance,

For she is her own.

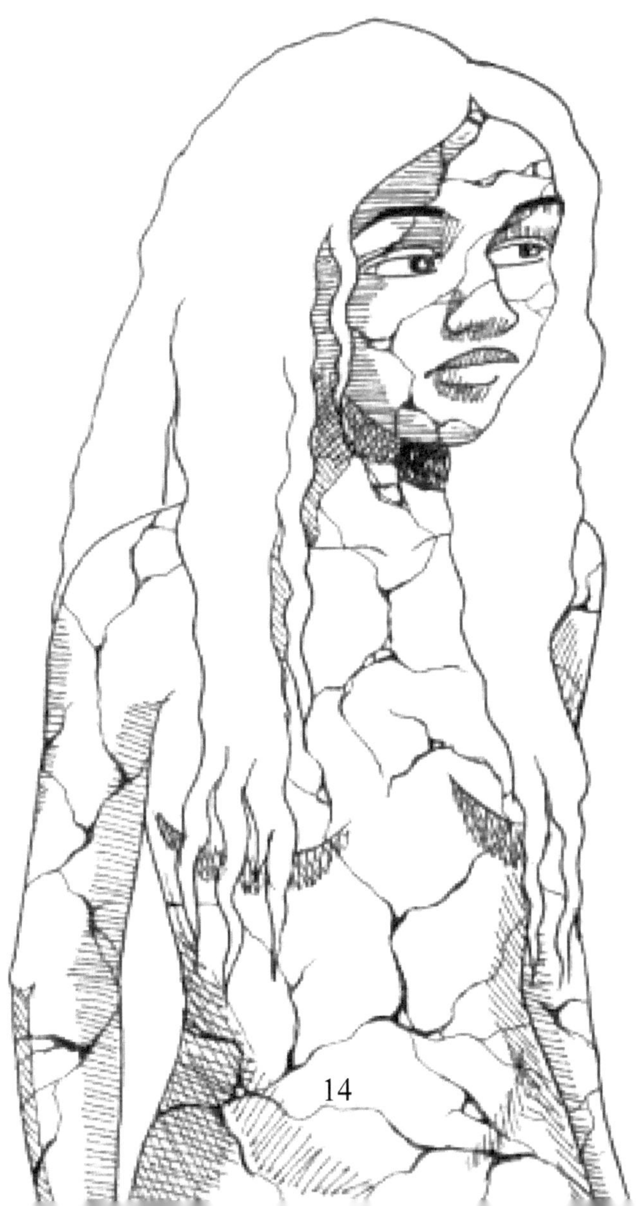

BHUVI TIBREWALLA

Parallel Choices

Our choices had always been the same,

When you choose the sunset,

I followed suit,

When you chased the sea,

I mirrored your pursuit.

When you looked at the moon,

I stared at it too.

When you picked yourself,

I chose you too.

As I said my dear,

Our choices had always been the same.

But with the twist in fate, my love

When I chose myself,

why did you hesitate to choose me too?

Inevitable

Life like the abyssal,

The never-ending, infinite, ongoing

It flows, clashes, and overlaps.

There are whales, sharks, and glaciers,

Despite these, it never stops,

It survives and it flows.

It flows like the sounds of the chatter,

the love in the air,

the blood in our veins,

And like the thoughts in one's mind.

It behaves like the aether,

Heavenly, vivid, melodramatic,

Like the sunsets and sunrises,

Stunning, simple, beautiful,

Yet so sightly.

As sightly as the change of the night,

The dimple of a newborn,

The stars in the sky,

And the dew on the blooming flower.

Life is like the cosmos,

Never-ending, infinite, ongoing,

Heavenly, vivid, melodramatic,

Flowing inevitably.

PATHWAYS

WITHIN

& with the faith in your heart, the obstacles

On your path will become your way.

~k.hpoetry

BHUVI TIBREWALLA

Thank You Mom

You Are A Daughter, A Sister,
An Aunt, And A Wife,
But Above All You Are,
A Mother Of A Great Kind.

We see you work,

Be it a day or night,

With the least rest and most interest,

You curate us all the time.

Thank You For Caring For Us The Most,
For Guiding Us When We Were Wrong,
Supporting Us When We Were Right,
For Loving Us Life Long.

Thank You For Shedding Your Tears For Us,
For Sharing Your Happiness, Joy With Us,
For Telling Us That We Are Special And Perfect,
And For Always Putting Your Trust In Us.

Yet we have failed to understand you,

To see past the smile on your lips,

To feel past the tiredness in your soul,

We failed to appreciate you.

Thank You For All The Compromises You Made,
And For The Scoldings You Gave Us,
Thank You For Always Being There,
And The Criticizations You Took For Us.

In the silent hours of dawn,

When the sun sets and the work dwells,

You stand still toiling and working,

Representing other women with their efforts
unseen.

Sorry For All The Complains And Troubles,
Please Stay With Us Forever,
The Words Above Are Less For You,
As You Are The Greatest Mother Ever!!

BHUVI TIBREWALLA

My Beloved Brother

It was the end of May,

But a new beginning,

For me, and for all,

And for that infant crying in that crib.

He had the same features,

He was alike to the new borns,

But yet,

He was different, he was speacial.

He hurled upon us as a blessing,

As a ray of light,

An emotion,

And an attachment.

He is the one I played with,

And I fought with,

He is the one who made me smile,

He is the one who wiped my tears every time I
cried.

He is too naïve,

That is what scares me,

The world will be too harsh with him,

But he'll have me

He keeps my secrets from every human alive,

He hears me blabber and rant till 3 at night,

He cries when I tease him, he cries when I cry,

People call him innocent, but only I know what
he is really like.

I don't want to end this, but I can't keep going

on,

I just want him to know,

"I am there for u even when u think I am not!"

Forever

You came into my life like an unknown face,

We shook hands unaware that it would be each other's hugs we would one day miss.

We laughed, and cried, and shared each other's pain,

And when everything changes, we ought to remain the same.

We didn't share genetics, or threads that bound us together,

We shared the trust, love, and loyalty that would be there forever.

We slept on the same bed, ate from the plate,

But now we die to stay at the same place.

We had our crying sessions at the drying stands,

We had our sneak-outs to the pavilion,

We had pink dinosaur moments,

We had our GRWM sessions,

We fought, we ignored, we overthought,

We grew apart,

But we always returned to each other,

No matter what the circumstances are.

If two fought, they would have gotten smacked.

We mess with others,

Cause we knew we had each other's back.

Cheers to our late-night talks,

Our LOC walks,

And our CDH songs,

These made our friendship so strong.

To the place that got us together,

All my gratitude to AVS,

You turned out to be my heaven,

The world revolves, and so do the people around us,

But we swore to the necklaces, T-shirts, and bracelets, that despite all changes,

We would remain constant throughout.

Enough with the past tenses,

I want you in my present and future,

You three will always have my back,

Be it earlier, now, or forever.

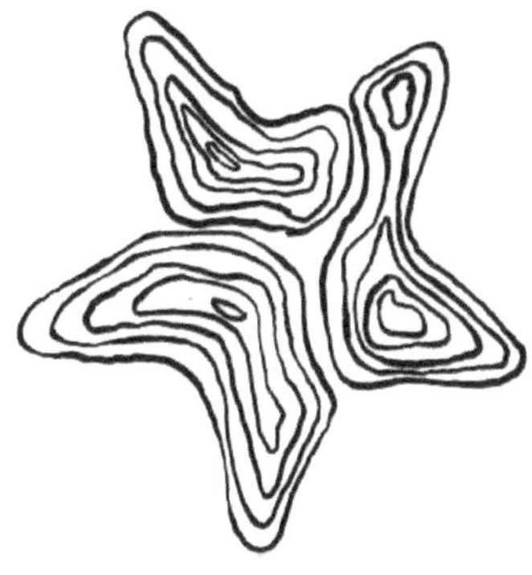

Papa

He is the one who keeps me breathing,

He is the one who keeps me smiling.

He calls me his doll, his princess, his little one,

He taught me lessons that were difficult to learn.

He is the one whom I'll call when I am in trouble,

He is the one who taught me to get out of my comfort bubble.

He lives my dreams with me,

He pushes me forward to get what I see.

He is my courage, my strength, and my confidence,

He is the reason for my will to succeed.

He is the one who hides his tears to give us capability,

He is the one who works day and night to provide us with our necessities.

He is someone who would have a smile on his face every time we see him,

Not knowing we can see the tiredness and pain in his eyes.

He is someone who might think I don't appreciate him enough,

But little does he know, his little angel never really grew up.

He is my light,

He is my fight,

He is the one who held my hand,

While I learned to take my flight.

He is the mountain that stands to protect me,

He is the river that flows with me,

He is the sky above that blesses me,

He is the soul I embrace within me.

And when the world pushes me around,

And I stumble on the ground,

He is the one who will hold my hand,

Clutch my fingers onto his palm,

And teach me to walk again.

He is the one in whose arms I find solace,

He is the one my heart withhold forever,

He is what everyone calls a girl's first love.

He is my dad, my papa, and my role model.

BHUVI TIBREWALLA

Tears In the Night

God saw you in pain,

So, he called you to him,

He wrapped his arms around you,

Saying, "Oh dear, come to me!"

You didn't deserve what you went through,

He gave you peace and rest.

But When I saw you there,

You laid lifeless.

You were free from the pain,

I could not help but wish,

Wish for hours for me to spend time with you,

I cried and cried and cried,

I wasn't ready for this,

But I knew now or later,

God would call you upon him.

You treated them all,

You made them all better.

You were always just a call away,

when we needed a doctor.

Now the lord has snatched that right,

From all of us,

As You have left us all,

In grief and sorrow.

None of us knew we had to let you go so soon.

Making that house feel less than a cocoon,

With us immediately running off to touch your
feet when we entered,

to now feeling your absence every time we encountered.

And thus, I would stand under the starry sky.

praying to God every night,

Asking him to let you come back,

But he wouldn't listen to me,

I would think "Why you?"

But then, you were the prettiest flower in the garden,

So, he picked you.

Don't worry Nanu,

We will be there on the terrace,

Every Sankranti flying kites,

Every birthday, anniversary, and festival,

Shouting and screaming under the same lights,

You will always be present with us,

In every joy, trouble, and sorrow

In the photos, memories and the hearts that are

now hollow.

Home

As the years passed,
people turned into homes,
some wrecked,
some shattered,
yet, remained my own.

I tried to mend what was broken,
tried to fix it,
but with the passing time,
and flowing people,
the wounds didn't heal—
they simply closed.

.

The homes I loved,

the homes I left,

they held a heartbeat,

It just did not beat for me

The homes remained,

wrecked and shattered.

The memories stayed,

nostalgic and regretful,

but the homes

had now become a house.

THE TAPESTRY

OF LIFE

Only when it is dark enough,

Can you see the stars.

~ Martin Luther King jr.

Are You Really Me?

I look in the mirror,

And wonder,

Who is the person I see?

Is it me?

Or is it the person the world wants to see?

I talk to the reflection,

But the voice I hear isn't mine,

I hear something different,

I hear the voice the world wants to hear ...

I look in the mirror,

And I see,

Someone looking just like me,

Is it my replica?

Or, is it me?

I look in the mirror,

And I see,

The smile on her lips,

The tears in her eyes,

hidden truths behind disguises.

Is the happiness just for the world to see?

I look and look and look,

And realize the tears down my cheeks,

The drops that tell me,

I am not the person I wanted to be….

I join palms with my "so-called" replica,

And ask hesitantly

In fervent whispers,

Are you… really me?

It Was a Beautiful Thing

It was a beautiful thing,

When we, two strangers met.

We shared our greetings,

Unaware of what the future held.

It was a beautiful thing,

When we became friends.

We spoke day and night,

Not knowing how this would end.

It was a beautiful thing,

When we resided our secrets in each other.

Calling each other friends,

But soon growing so much farther.

It was a beautiful thing,

When we were in each other's DMs.

But now a text is something,

That we even hesitate to send.

It was a beautiful thing,

When we at least called each other friends.

But now,

We know that everything has an end.

It was a beautiful thing,

It was pure,

It was only friendship,

With nothing more involved.

It was a beautiful thing,

When we met beside the lawn,

But now you post reels,

With the ones you know now.

It was a beautiful thing,

Our friendship, bond, and trust.

But now it's all crushed.

With our chats deleted,

Our places were wiped,

You went on with your new friends,

While I went on with mine.

But now it is similar to the circle of life,

Where we are strangers to each other again,

Suddenly stopped talking to each other,

Was the method we used to move away.

Scrolling like we don't care,

Unknown of what went wrong and where,

Drowning in our thoughts,

Figuring out if we had given our best?

Slowly but gradually, it did happen

For us, or for our other relationships,

We decided to ruin,

The beautiful thing that we had.

Alone

I was there,

ALONE

In the dark,

Surrounded by mirrors,

Mirrors, that stared back at me,

Whispers and murmurs that surrounded me.

I could see Reflections,

Reflection I was unknown to,

I stepped back and so did they,

I lift my right hand,

They did too,

Except

THE ROCK I THREW,

here was a loud silence after,

With me on the floor,

The whispers silenced,

And the reflection,

CRACKED

AND

SHATTERED

The silenced whispers,

That now turned to screams,

Screams of chaos within me.

However,

I stood there still,

In the dark

ALONE

AND

DIMMED

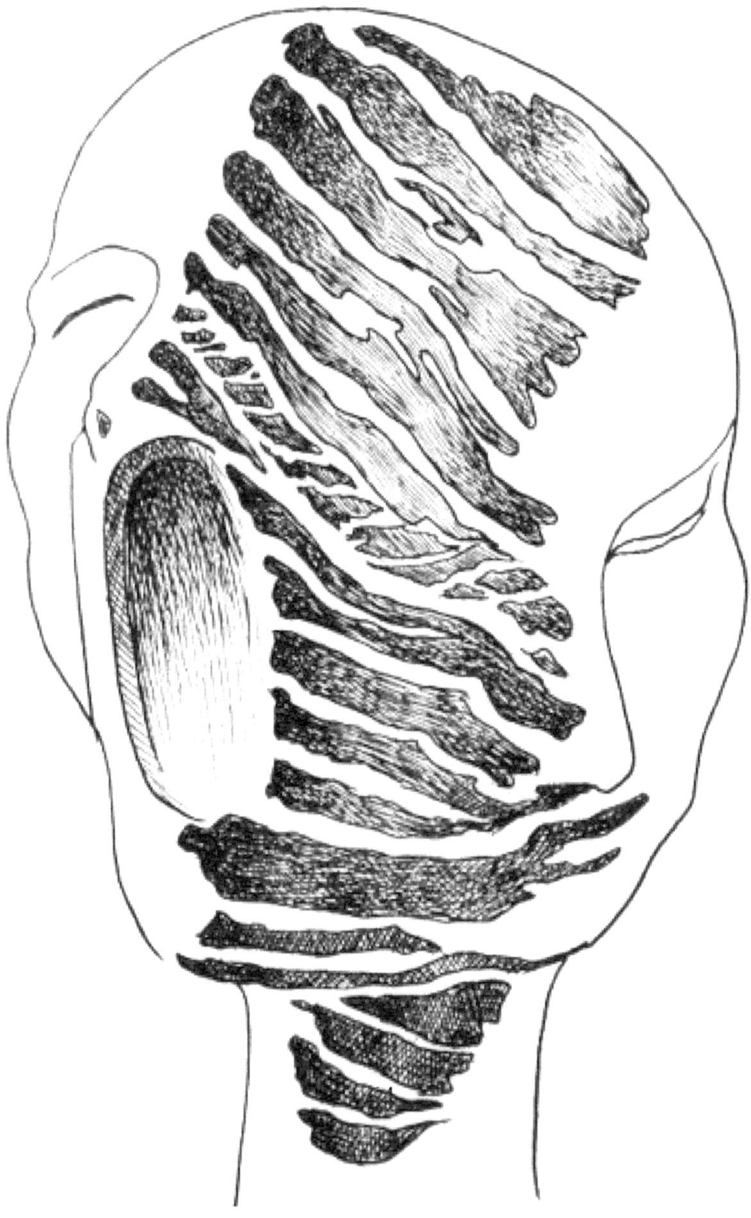

The Drops of Love

When the drops fell from a starry sky,

It felt like a sparkle,

It felt like a blessing,

It felt unknown, it felt exciting,

It felt scary, It felt hard,

But then I looked up

AND

It was you

Love was then easy,

It was beautiful,

It was sweet, it was fun,

It was wild, it was risky,

It was fascinating, it was homely,

It was the hug, it was the word,

It was the kiss, it was the fight,

It was like the drop of rain, on a starry night.

Would you?

Would you call me crazy?

If I tell you I miss the roads,

I miss the trees, the grass, and the scents.

If I tell you I miss the handprints, lanterns,

The decoration and the events.

Would you call me crazy?

If I tell you I miss the classrooms,

The canteens, auditorium, and complexes,

If I tell you I miss the teachers, exams and the

didis.

Would you call me crazy?

If I tell you I miss the late-night walks, the mid-night talks

I miss the raids and the change in breaks,

If I tell you I miss standing in dining hall lines,

I miss getting dressed on the way when never on time.

Would you call me crazy?

If I tell you I miss the hillocks, the pavilion,

I miss the statues and the sculptures

If I tell you I miss the sneak-outs and the fun.

I miss my friends and the hide-and-seek.

Would you call me crazy?

If I tell you I miss every little thing about that place,

I miss the raindrops, the sun's rays and the autumn leaves.

If I tell you I am still not used to this change.

Would you call me crazy?

I tell you I left the place that embraced my teen,

Doing it all for my dream,

If I tell you I wonder if doing it was all worth it,

Leaving it all behind, for something uncertain.

Would you call me crazy?

If I tell you there is no place like it you will ever find.

I left it with board paper in my hand,

With our suitcases packed,

Cakes were cut, and polaroids clicked,

We left it with tears in our eyes.

Would you still call me crazy if I told you these?

Beneath the silence

Caressing my hair,
My mom kissed me goodnight,
"Sleep before the monsters come out," she said.

Maybe the monsters weren't under my bed,
But inside my head.
The ones we feared at night,
Did we become like them?

In the dark room,
That mirrors our heart,
Screaming and crying,
Yet silence echoed all around.

My trembling lips,

Ripping at my hair,
Unaware of what to do,
I took the blade in my hand.

And just like this,
My story remained incomplete,
With the darkness around,
And the monsters within,
I let the fear consume me.

76

ACKNOWLEDGEMENT

I would like to express my deepest gratitude to Keya Tiwari and Annanya Periwal, whose artistic talents have brought my poetry to life. Keya's beautiful illustrations for The Celestial Night, The World I Live In, Parallel Choices, Inevitable, Thank You Mom, Beloved Brother, Forever, Papa, Home, Pathways Within, Tapestry of Life, Discovering Horizons, Drops of Love, and Beneath the Silence perfectly capture the essence of each poem. Keya also designed the striking cover page that gives this book its visual identity.

Annanya's incredible work on Infinite Mirrors of Belief, She, Tears in the Night, Are You Really Me, It Was a Beautiful Thing, Alone, and Would You add a powerful dimension to these pieces. Though the initial inspirations for these illustrations were drawn from Pinterest and Google, each work was entirely sketched and developed by their skilful hands.

To my family and friends, your constant encouragement and unwavering support have been the backbone of this journey. Thank you for standing by me through every step of this creative process.

This book would not have been possible without all of you. Thank you from the bottom of my heart.

79

80

So many words became songs and poetries,

but they still fell short to express the

thoughts unspoken....

BHUVI TIBREWALLA